CLIMATE CHANGE
Effects on Turtles

By Leilani Hale

I0163194

Library For All Ltd.

Threats to Turtles

Cyclones can be deadly to sea turtles and other animals. Cyclones are powerful storms that form over warm tropical waters, driven by hot, humid weather conditions.

The hot air rising sucks in more air, which builds into a spiral of clouds and rain.

A cyclone can reach up to 290 kph wind speed.

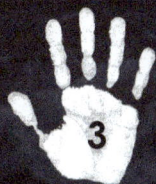

3

How Cyclones Affect Turtles and Community

Cyclones bring heavy rain and often trigger other natural disasters, like floods and landslides. These cause silt, sand and rubbish to build up on the ocean floor.

Seagrass and turtle habitats suffer. The pollution washed into the ocean by landslides damages turtles' food sources and their homes, filling them with silt and dirt.

When cyclones damage land and sea, communities feel the pain it has caused to Country and find it disheartening. Losing homes, important possessions, and sometimes even lives is devastating to people. It's important to be resilient and stay hopeful during disasters.

DID YOU KNOW?

Cyclones can wash marine animals ashore, injuring and affecting their population.

They also dump debris and rubbish onto beach shores and coral reefs, damaging turtle habitats and breeding grounds.

Cyclones also cause erosion on beaches, which affects the survival rate of turtle eggs.

How Cyclones Damage Seagrass Meadows

The increase in heavy storms and cyclones, caused by climate change, has led to dirt and harmful minerals entering the ocean. This has severely impacted the sea turtle's main food source: seagrass.

Due to the sand, dirt, and pollutants that enter the ocean during cyclones, seagrass beds are buried under layers of sediment and rubbish. This blocks the sunlight, making it harder for grasses to grow.

Seagrass is important because it's the main food for many sea animals, especially sea turtles. It also helps keep the ocean clean by producing oxygen and filtering out pollutants.

Seagrass Ecosystem Changes from Indigenous Perspectives

Seagrass beds are recognised as a nursery site for sea life. Traditional owners change fishing and gathering practices to suit the seasons. But sand movement and sediment has caused seagrass destruction, which changes breeding patterns. Some seagrass meadows regenerate, but many have been destroyed by increased cyclones and flooding.

Sightings of turtles have declined with the destruction of seagrass meadows.

The Sea Turtle's Challenges

Turtles cannot find food when the seagrass beds are covered in cyclone debris. They then have to travel further from home to find food. This journey can be exhausting and sometimes too much for the turtle's health to handle.

Seagrass beds take several years to grow back after a flood incident.

Eating seagrass helps turtles stay healthy.

Floating Turtle Syndrome

Floating Turtle Syndrome has been observed by Indigenous communities on sea Country, especially after cyclones. It happens when too much sand buries the seagrass and turtles accidentally eat it while searching for food. Traditional practices include rescuing and rehabilitating floating turtles.

Eating sand causes blockages and leads to gas build-up, so the turtles end up floating.

Effects on Turtles

The Indigenous Perspective on Sea Turtle Ecology and Cyclone Yasi

Indigenous observation notes that sea turtles may change their feeding patterns and migrate to different areas when their usual feeding grounds are damaged by cyclones.

Cyclone Yasi was one of the most powerful cyclones ever recorded in Australia. It made landfall in northern Queensland in 2011, causing major destruction.

After Cyclone Yasi, there was a major decline in turtle numbers. Elders decided that hunting should be limited to give the turtle population time to regenerate. This is called a 'moratorium,' and has been in place for many years in some areas.

Rangers monitor turtles, and can rescue or re-home them as needed while their food source regrows.

Scientific Insights on Turtle Conservation

Studies show that cyclones, and the flooding they bring can damage sea turtle populations. The storms can destroy the beaches where turtles lay their eggs, and the flooding can ruin the seagrass beds where they feed. This makes it harder for turtles to survive and for baby turtles to hatch and grow up safely.

The whole marine environment relies on seagrass for health!

Indigenous Perspectives on Turtle Ecosystem Changes

Changes that have occurred in Indigenous sea country over thousands of years have been passed on to the next generation through stories. Because climate change is a newer problem, there are no older traditional insights about it, only recent management practices.

However, the current struggles of seagrasses, turtles, and other marine animals will be represented in future stories and art. The stories will illustrate how some traditional customs have been threatened by climate change.

Turtles are very important to traditional owners, and we continue to look after them, our land, and our sea country for the future generations.

Cultural Impacts and Stories

The turtle is an important feature in Indigenous culture and stories. There are Dreamtime stories about the creation of turtles, and turtles have been an important resource for thousands of years. As climate change threatens them, Indigenous rangers have worked hard to keep this ancient and crucial creature safe.

Traditional art of turtles can be found all over Australia.

Helping Hands for Turtles

Conservationists work hard to protect turtles, especially during cyclone season. They help by rebuilding damaged beaches so turtles can lay their eggs, and by planting more seagrass to make sure turtles have enough to eat. They also keep an eye on turtle health and help rescue turtles that are in trouble after storms.

There are also many moratoriums in place regarding sea turtles. Rangers monitor the turtle populations, as well as cultural indicators and the shift in the seasons. Everything is recorded in databases, and government conservationists work closely with Traditional Owners and Elders.

DID YOU KNOW?

Conservationists are trying many methods to help turtles survive climate change.

Sea turtles are some of the world's most ancient creatures. They've been around since the dinosaurs!

Sea turtles can hold their breath under water for hours. But when they are stressed, like after a storm, this ability is compromised.

Turtles also struggle to eat when they are stressed, which is also a problem during cyclones.

Turtles are very good at adapting to change. They are survivors! But they still need healthy oceans to thrive.

How You Can Help Protect the Turtles!

The best way to help the turtles is to get involved.

If you get involved in conservation efforts, you can symbolically adopt a turtle!

Reduce, Reuse, Recycle! Keeping rubbish out of the ocean helps turtles stay safe.

Go to beach clean-ups and make sure you take your rubbish home with you when you visit.

Learning more about turtles and volunteering with local conservation groups is very helpful.

Share what you've learned! Friends, family, and classmates are just waiting to hear all about turtles.

If you're allowed, use social media to spread awareness. You can post with the #SaveTheTurtles and #OceanConservation hashtags.

Stay up to date with turtle news through websites like CSIRO and the Marine Conservation Society!

Photo Credits

Page	Attribution
Cover	Photo courtesy of the Queensland Indigenous Land and Sea Ranger Program.
Pages 2-3	Kirienko Oleg/Shutterstock.com
Page 4	Rich Carey/Shutterstock.com
Page 5	Ashish_wassup6730/Shutterstock.com
Page 6 (above)	Mike Workman/Shutterstock.com
Page 6 (below)	Andriy Nekrasov/Shutterstock.com
Page 7	vikilikov/Shutterstock.com
Page 8	Shahar Shabtai/Shutterstock.com
Page 9 (above)	The Urban Tropic/Shutterstock.com
Page 9 (below)	Photo courtesy of the Queensland Indigenous Land and Sea Ranger Program.
Page 11	Public Domain
Page 12	Photo courtesy of the Queensland Indigenous Land and Sea Ranger Program.
Page 13 (above)	© Library For All
Page 13 (below)	Photo courtesy of the Queensland Indigenous Land and Sea Ranger Program.
Page 14	Xavier Hoenner/Shutterstock.com
Page 15 (both)	Photos courtesy of the Queensland Indigenous Land and Sea Ranger Program.
Pages 16-17	Photo courtesy of the Queensland Indigenous Land and Sea Ranger Program.
Page 18	Photo courtesy of the Queensland Indigenous Land and Sea Ranger Program.
Pages 20-21	Photo courtesy of the Queensland Indigenous Land and Sea Ranger Program.

You can use these questions to talk about this book with your family, friends and teachers.

What did you learn from this book?

Describe this book in one word. Funny? Scary? Colourful? Interesting?

How did this book make you feel when you finished reading it?

What was your favourite part of this book?

Download the Library For All Reader app from libraryforall.org

Queensland Indigenous Land and Sea Ranger Program

The Queensland Indigenous Land and Sea Ranger Program collaborates with First Nations communities to protect and care for land and sea Country. With over 200 rangers, the program shares cultural knowledge, engages in community education, and leads youth programs like the Junior Ranger initiative, fostering a strong connection to Country and Culture.

Leilani Hale is a Yuku-baja-Muliku Ranger from Cooktown community.

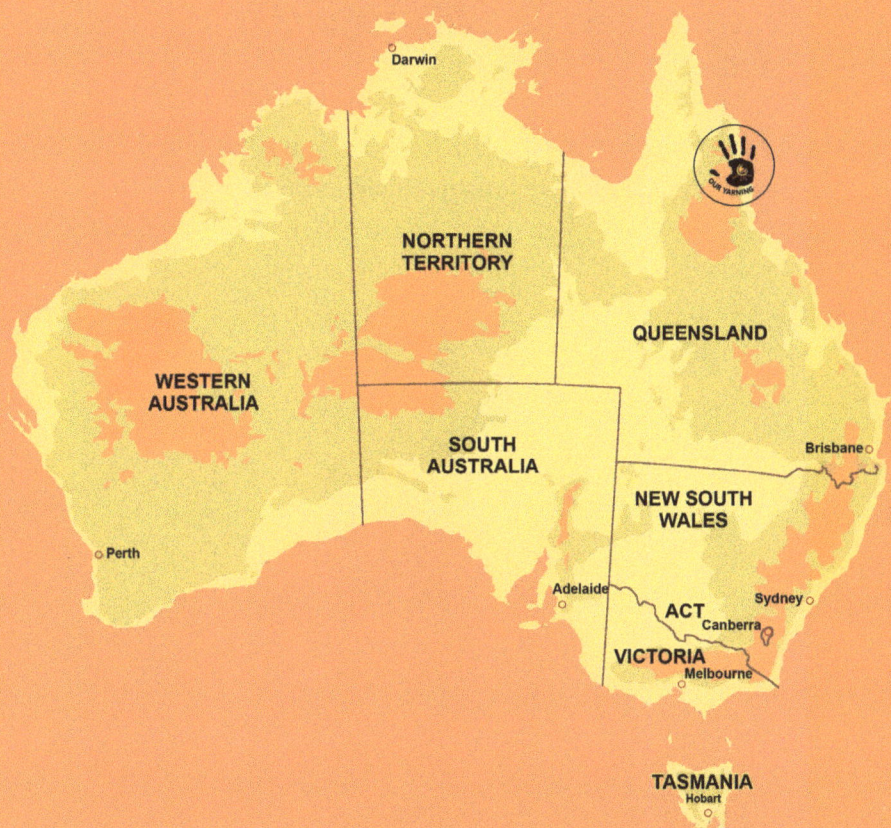

Our Yarning

The Our Yarning collection aligns with the Australian Curriculum through the Cross-Curriculum Priorities — Aboriginal and Torres Strait Islander Histories and Cultures. The collection provides an authentic opportunity for learning and embedding Aboriginal and Torres Strait Islander perspectives because it is written by Aboriginal and Torres Strait Islander people.

We know that children learn better, and enjoy reading more, when they see themselves in the stories, characters and illustrations of the books they read.

To download the app, visit the Google Play Store or Apple Store and search 'Our Yarning'.

libraryforall.org

You're reading Upper Primary

Learner – Beginner readers

Start your reading journey with short words,
big ideas and plenty of pictures.

Level 1 – Rising readers

Raise your reading level with more words,
simple sentences and exciting images.

Level 2 – Eager readers

Enjoy your reading time with familiar words,
but complex sentences.

Level 3 – Progressing readers

Develop your reading skills with creative stories
and some challenging vocabulary.

Level 4 – Fluent readers

Step up your reading skills with playful narratives,
new words and fun facts.

Middle Primary – Curious readers

Discover your world through science and stories.

Upper Primary – Adventurous readers

Explore your world through science and stories.

Library For All is an Australian not for profit organisation with a mission to make knowledge accessible to all via an innovative digital library solution.
Visit us at libraryforall.org

Climate Change: Effects on Turtles

First published 2024

Published by Library For All Ltd
Email: info@libraryforall.org
URL: libraryforall.org

This project was delivered with the support of QBE under the Community Ready partnership.

This book was made possible with the support of the Queensland Indigenous Land and Sea Ranger Program to support educational outcomes for children in Australia by learning from Indigenous knowledge and stewardship of Country. To learn more, visit https://www.qld.gov.au/environment/plants-animals/conservation/community/land-sea-rangers/locations.

Our Yarning logo design by Jason Lee, Bidjipidji Art

Climate Change: Effects on Turtles
Hale, Leilani
ISBN: 978-1-923376-15-1
SKU04437